TRUTH AND OTHER PRECIOUS THINGS

By
Roger C Horton

```
I0190780
```

October 2020 Second Edition
Original, December 2001 First Edition

Copyright © by Roger C Horton

All rights reserved by the author

ISBN 9780990680833

CONTENTS

3

Author's Note

I enjoy old proverbs, wisdom and humor in a few short words. There is always a point to be made. Of course, I have my favorites. Here are a few examples:

The devil is not wise because he's the devil; he's wise because he's old.

Every man is the hero of his own story. We get too soon old and too late smart. Life may be short but it can also be wide.

I believe poetry must also make a point or show us a bit of truth. Big words and style are secondary to truth. Poetry is very personal, so if you are touched by only a few of these poems I've done my job. I hope you and I together share a bit of truth.

R. Charles Horton

Waste Not

Upon a sterile strip of rock, man made.
A street, a pressing, pulsing live cascade,
Here a wrinkled ancient wreck, I brushed.
And with a bony claw was grasped,
Oh look, I am yourself, he rasped,
The place toward which you rush, he gasped.
Waste not! You fool, waste not!

    His grip, it was a taloned vice.
    I pried at it; I was not nice.
    Then it was, our eyes did meet.
    Said he, this tomb beneath our feet,
    Spins away, a day, a day away
    In tacit suddenness--- what? no other day.
    One moment life, it goes---to dark repose

Then in the embers of his eyes,
Visions, my life, its empty lies
Locked in his grip, locked in his stare,
Truth lay me down; it striped me bare.
The orbs, now iridescent pools,
The sea, the stars through forest trees,
Children's laughs, in summer breeze.

    He blinked, door shut, curtain fell.
    Words of passion broke the spell.
    The essence of each instant grasp.
    Spend every moment as your last.
    His head, he twist it all awry,
    Heard silent sounds, a silent cry.
    At my feet, I watched him die.

                    Waste Not!

Differences

Dogs and cats.
Diplomats.
Republicans and democrats.
So many groups get really pissed,
Like miners with ecologists.
Some racial views can really vex.
Scholars tangle over text.
But no greater hate is in effect,
Than 'tween holy men----
                    Of different sect

INSANE

Emotionally in pain,
Love fell on them like rain.
Their wills went down the drain.
They were mutually insane.

Conforming to the social main,
They vowed to so remain,
Thus, from reason to abstain,
For life---
                totally **INSANE.**

AN ODE TO EXCELLENCE

Ah - excellence has varied form,
And for the arts, there is no norm,
So, compliments to artists of all kind.
Painters, sculptors, writers, masters of the rhyme,
Dancers, movie makers, singers all sublime,
All performing actors, lusting for the lime,
Even sleazy con men, angling for a dime.
The medics and nurses, you pay to feel fine,
Hear your dour preacher, advise on things divine.
Carpenters and farmers, soldiers on the line,
Cooks or chefs whatever, on whose cuisine we dine,
Kids who un-nerve us, with calculated whine.
Hookers, real experts, of the bump and grind,
Gigolos for whom, Rich widows pant and pine,
Why even the base burglar can be artistic with a crime.
Professional spokes persons that who events define.
Political writers, whose words adjust our minds,
Aired by big shot speakers, who try to talk us blind.
And --the devil too should have his due;
He's been at it a long time.
So, a bow to all the maestros,
A hand for efforts fine,
And even recognition though unkind --
For those skilled as an Equine - - **Behind!**

So tired

A woman,
She had once belonged to a man.
She - now independent, is a mother of children,

Children – for whom she takes all responsibility,
Everyday planning for the following day,
For the next month and year ..... responsible
For their education, health, morals ..... responsible
For every facet of their own, her own being---responsible
She knows herself to be responsible
She endeavors and she does succeed in being
responsible
Yet always, always,
Her success seems to totter on the brink of failure,
And though she endures, she is tired---
                                        So tired!

What she wants is a reasonable happiness.
Her wish is for a little happiness,
For herself, for her children to be happy.
Within themselves, for their spirit to be happy.
These goals seem reasonable, seem possible,
Yet somehow conflict with what's possible.
What seems so simple ...... is it possible?
        Yet always, always,
Happiness has seemed reasonable and possible,
But she is tired of trying to create happiness—

                                So tired!

Often, she has thought, …. if she only had a man,
A man who would give her rest,
And she would make him happy.
She would strive as a woman to make him happy.
       And of course, she could make her darling
happy
       And her children would also be happy.
Yet before … she had strived to love a man
And strived until it exhausted her.
And strived until her whole self had begun to
dissolve,
        Yet always, always,
She strived, even though her effort went down and
down
And she had sunk into black despair, …..
                                        So tired!

Why could she not achieve this?
To make one other being happy and she remain
happy?
It seemed to her so … so possible,
With a little more effort …… possible,
With some small sacrifice on her part …… possible,
By offering up, letting go of another piece of herself
… possible.
It had not been so simple as that.

Yet always, always,
She had strived to make it possible,
And she had become tired, tired, ...

So tired!

There is a man, a new man,
For a new man is always possible.
A new man who would offer to her his support.
A new man who would plan for her, be responsible
for her support.
A new man who would have her ...... please him for
that support.
Yet she could rest in him, and she was tired.
She could give it up, the planning, the striving, the
responsibility.
She could give herself over to the man.
But men need more than love; they need surrender.
To their own striving, some men demand surrender.
The man would expect her life to meld into his.
The man would expect her will to dissolve into his,
So that she no longer thought, questioned, strived,
So that she no longer was, ... was .... herself,
Yet always, always,
She had remained conscious of whom she was,
And yet she had become very tired, ...

So tired!

It was as if a woman allowed herself to be
submerged,
By a man, beneath the surface of the sea -
submerged,
Sharing a hose through which they breathed in life -
submerged.
Through love and trust, she allows herself to sink.
Held in the man's arms, she allows herself to sink.
Sharing life through a slender hose - submerged.
By his very size and his masculine need, he takes
more air,
But for her there remains sufficient air.
She gladly survives on what he allows her,
        Yet always, always,
She is aware of what he allows her,
And of this awareness, she becomes tired, ...
                                    So tired!

For some men this is not enough.
For some men this proportionate equality is not
enough.
They would take more air, and more.
They might leave her gasping, even pinching it off,
Suffocating her sense of self to enhance their
power.

Held so by commitments, by fear,
Held so by the constraints of society,
She cannot breathe; she withers.
Her conscious self, frantic to survive longs, to break
free,
Break the surface, rise thus not perish.
Should she struggle, rise, allow her sense of self to
breathe?
Should she struggle to drink in the chill air of
independence?
Should she yield---let her spirit sleep---commit---
submit?
Should she---disappear within him?
          Yet always, always,
He would strive to make her no more than---just---
what he wishes,
And of his striving, she is tired---
                              So tired!

There are men. There are always men.
There are some who would embrace her sense of
self.
There must be some who would coexist with her
sense of self.
Yet she does not know which men and what man.
And she is tired, so tired of everything.
And she only wants to be happy.

And she only wants to make one dear person
happy.
And the man---who wants her to belong,
Who wants her to belong to him, rest in him,
His price for that rest---is that she must disappear
into him.
She is already disappearing, for her shadow is pale.
Yet always, always,
She has always known, though it becomes difficult
to remember---
       Who she is---
           being tired---
               So tired!

She must decide, for she needs to be happy,
And she needs to make one dear person happy,
And needs to see her children happy,
And she needs a man's rest to be happy,
And she understands that there is somewhere a man,
And she has dreamed, sensed somewhere a man.
A man, who would embrace her independent spirit,
A man, who would rejoice in her woman's spirit,
A man, who would give rest, to that spirit,
A man, who she must seek out,
Who she must find to be happy,
And the man now, who would have her belong,
He would strive to make her less than her pale shadow,
And though she understands, though she is frightened,
She is tired of being frightened and she is just tired.

  Yet always, always,
There is so much that must be done,
and far more must be done to be happy,
And she is tired of doing---her spirit is tired---
      So tired!

ANTILLES

Below the trades...Antilles,
Of the tropic mountain vales,
Isles afloat in blue coral seas.
Awash with life, under, over,
Swirling, thru gardens, multicolor,
Gardens green in tone and texture,
Green in every vein and mixture,
Brushed with purple, red rust luster,
Bearing fruits in yellow cluster.
Like magic from the very air,

Rain drops glisten everywhere.
Water springs, thru rock, bubbling.
Water---falls, through rainbows misting.
Water flows, past children laughing,
Through caverns---of cathedral trees.

There, from games running. . . Arawak.
Gentile folk of cassava of sweet sop,
Planters of the maize, the plantain,
Hunting mapuri, and fishes,

Workers, cotton, stone and shell,
Beneath the sun, Arawadi seeing,
Happy in the art of being.
Old ones live, till spirits sleep.
Young ones live, and old ways keep.
Balance between the earth and sky,
Each thing that lives, must also die.

Fierce, men of prey...Carib.
Fierce, god of storm...Huracan,
Tears from earth the mighty tree,
Carib canoes, flash from the sea.
Winds in their fury and their length,
Shake the world with fearsome strength,
Storms of arrows, darts, and stones,
Take heads and eat the flesh and bones.

Spirits lost and women's moans,
Asks of the sun, "What have we done?"
Good to live, but all must die,
Balance of the earth and sky.
Fierce storms that come to go,
Natures rhythm, natures flow.

South from Caicos...caravel.
Upon white dorsal, lateen sail,
Blood red cross of the true god,
Suns glint on hauberk, on mail.
South from Caicos...Christobol.
By the will of god, let mercy reign,
Borne with seal of sovereign Spain,
For souls, and gold, to the Asian Main.
Glory, power, social gain,
Those to follow would remain,
Upon the garden shore...Christobal.

Piercing the green veil...steel.
Rust stained hidalgos, of good weal,
Sweating, tore at fern and flowered walls,
Slash and burn the forest halls.
In loathsome pits, captives crawl,
Mining gold until they fall.
Up from the coast...caballeros,
Swept cool rivers, horse and hound,
Through lush valley, hunt men down,
Run los Indios to the ground.
Gods wrath upon the mountain rolls.
Chastise for Christ the heathen souls.
Sword and lance, woman and child,
Old and young, their bodies piled.
Gold, lust, holy zeal defiled.
Storms of flame and musket cracks.
Cruel whips flay the last brown backs.
Gone from the forest...Arawak.

West from Africa...Slavers.
Out from the Gambia, Niger, Cameroon,
Guinea coast to Indies barracoon,
Black flesh, for sugar and doubloon.
Deep laden, bodies crammed, sweat drenched,
Spoon stowed, naked on each bench,
Mad of thirst, they cannot quench,
Moans rise up through hate and stench.
West toward Antilles...mercy god,
A good wind, and fair, and haste,
Death, pestilence, and oozing waste.

The living squirm chained to the dead.
Sick splashed astern, and lean sharks fed.
Port with but half---served profits need,
Then endless toil---black seed.

Fraught with avarice---sovereigns---
Envious of Indies wealth,
Did plot and scheme with greedy stealth.
With boldness, each meant to attain,
These isles off the Spanish Main,
Where countless slaves but lived to sow,
Fields of coffee, sugar, indigo.
Merchant, pirate, man o' war,
Like sharks into Antilles bore,
And in their lust, and in their pride,
Many fought, and many died.
Cutlass and canon, smashed and tore,
Full on, three hundred years or four----
Until exhausted---sick of more---
The slaves rose up, bathed them in gore.

Out from field and pen...rebellion.
Swift as limber lightning fell,
Stabs and blows and snarling hell,
Avenge, burn, rape and kill,
Those slow to flee, live not to tell.
Militias stand, grow and drill,
Prepare to fight and to repel---
Armies that come, but cannot quell,
The rage for freedom, and the will.

Through the carnage...gardens grew.
As nations change, so peoples too.
Wind bent palms line the strand,
Green slopes of the hinterlands.
Slow tilts the balance...of the mass,
Plows scrape away the highland grass.
Forest fall to burn charcoal.
Dead earth slides, and rivers shoal.
Rain becomes brown roaring flood.
Reefs are choked with silt and mud.
The rhythms of the earth's green buds.
Gone nature's wondrous...primitive.

Look high along the Carib...beach,
Farther than the eye can reach,
Fenced bastions of the rich elite,
Hotel, facades, and thick concrete.
Ports that feed this great machine,
From needs no one now can wean,
Governed with vain prerogative,
There's little left to take or give.

Thus, boats cast off Antilles shore,
Crewed by the ragged hungry poor,
West on the trades, short hope in store,
Down reef strewn island corridor.
Hunger, thirst, and tropic storms,
Wrecks, death, terror, still they swarm.

The balance of the earth and sky.
All that lives, must also die.
And so passes into history...

When---your last garden---**Antilles?**

BURN

Hot sky, a **cool** grove, weak panting breezes.
Strong tree, it's **deep** shade, out of he gazes.
Burn Sun, on **hot** clay, walking she passes.
Cool breeze, she's **cool** fire, his vision blazes.

Burn down, **hot** sky, her pounding heart races.
Cool shade, **strong** tree, her eyes he
embraces.
Hot Sun, **spare** me, this heat that rises.
Cool wind, **fan** me, dampen my senses.

Fire's heat, **smoke's** heat, from shade he's
emerging.
Cool heat, **ice** heat, her body melting.
Hot heat, **fire's** heat, **air's** heat breathing.
Cool Ice, **quench** fire, there's no enduring.

Hot Sun, **strong** man, beauty's set flaming.
Cool Ice, **hot** shade, can't fight her wanting.
Burn fire, **burn** ice, wild passion smoking.
Ice hot, **heat** blast, each other's yearning.

Man fire, **burn** me, **seize** me, **please** me!
Hot shade, **melt** me, **scald** me, **ease** me!
Burn Sun, **burn** sky, don't coolly **tease** me!
White heat, **loves** heat, flaming **appease** me!

MOON

Moon---
   Night's cool mirror of the day,
Shades with misty bolts of silver gray,
   Cast through halo-ed clouds,
Reflections play.
   We speak hush voiced,
And feel---Fae.

BUT HE DON'T HEAR ME

Could the calendar be wrong?
God it seems so awfully long.
Since I came to be with him.
Came here alone with him.
I speak, he just don't hear.
I speak his minds somewhere.
He talks; I hear each word.
Listen; know what I've heard.
I hear all that he needs.
He tells me how he bleeds.
But he don't hear me try.
Don't know I'm gonna die.

I remember, its absurd
Every lie and hurtful word
And though he doesn't hear me
He often swears he loves me
Brings home the daily bread
And takes me to his bed
Within I feel the way
His words cut every day
Says, I don't like your friend
You're not seeing her again
Or you're not working there
Or! Hey! What's with your hair?
Girl you're looking fat
Who said to dress like that?
You're made up like a whore
My God you're such a bore
And who told you to think
You're such a silly dink
Why'd you smile at my friend?
Are you playing round again?
Hey! You don't need your car
You can easy walk that far.

He speaks of mighty deeds
And the sort of job he needs
But he don't hear me cry
Wouldn't think to wonder why

My god, the walls are near
I need another beer
I smoke, I drink, I pray
Just to stay another day
Because… I love him
I don't want to hurt him

Well, I walked away last week.
And he called me very meek.
Said, but babe I love you.
But babe I need you.
Oh, babe you hurt me.
Why did you leave me?
And you can call your friend.
When you come back again.
I promise not to fight.
That stupid jobs all right.
The bills are such a mess.
And I love the way you dress.
You can have the car.
I'll spend less time at the bar.
I'll be home instead.
I miss you in my bed.
Cause babe I love you.
Cause babe I need you.

You can't just hurt me.
You can't just leave me.

First he sounded sad
Then he got so mad
Said, he knew it in his gut
I was just another slut
I tell him how I feel
To him it isn't real
I speak, he just don't hear
I speak, he's just not there
Says, Babe I love you
Says, Please I love you
Sure! ... he wants me
Needs to have me------
        But-----He doesn't hear me.

CALM

Calm---
  So calm.
Image of the sky upon the swell.
Calm---
  So calm.
Listen to the whale's song;
    Hear the dolphin tell,
Of Tempest---
  Soon to make this frothy hell.

CLOUDS

Clouds as soaring mountains, desert dune,
As living breathing things traverse the sky,
 And clothe the rain-bowed sphere with veils a-fly.
These changelings of myriad shape and hue,
 With light they twist and ply,
Our moods with glooms and glories they imbue---
  And up at them we gaze and sigh.

Fog

Fog---
　　Obscuring all the world in night and day.
Shroud---
　　Pierced by the prow, bleeds swirls of gray.
Wraths---
　　Listen with your eyes to hear them say,
Of---
　　Deadly perils in the walls of gray.

NIGHT WATCH

Starry, starry night,

Dark Opal, dimly bright,

Black water, foaming white,

Past this shell of warmth and light.

Keep vigilant amidst the ocean's might.

STORM

Storm----Spawned of heat and cold so far away,
Born as raging wind, the clouds to flay,
Marching, tumbling seas in vast array,
To pound and wrack our ship,
　　　　　　　　　And make us pray.

CYCLES

Under a dark sky.
A snowflake falling.
One upon another.
White carpet extending.
High mounds piling.
Blowing drifts onward.
Over rock under.
Drops trickle flowing.
To the sea falling.
A warm mist rising.
Under a dark sky

SEA STRUCK

Beneath the dome of the sky.
Before far horizon, stretches sea.
Before blue depth lay emerald shoal.
Before ocher froth, white dazzle of sand.

Where on Proceeding his shadow he stood,
Amazed that this magic could,
Call forth such wondrous fear,
And elude him to his present year.

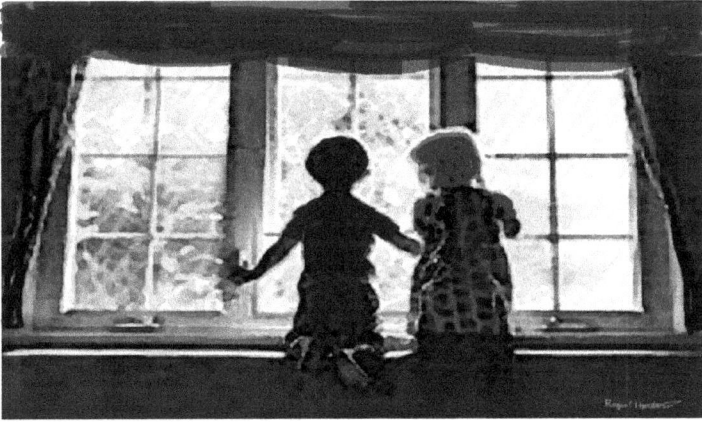

FALLING RAIN

Clouds gray rolling, clouds of rain.
Eyes turn upward, in disdain.
Run, run thither, shelter gain.
Clouds gray sweeping, falling rain.

Sky so changeless, watch the rain.
Seek the sunshine, seek in vain.
Child's face to the, windowpane.
Clouds gray dreary, falling rain.

On the rooftop, hear the rain.
Pit pat tip tap, like a train.
Sound of gurgling, down the drain.
Clouds gray hazy, falling rain.

Water dripping, drip drop rain.
Little ones fidget, they complain.
Pitter patter, going insane.
Clouds gray gloomy----falling rain.

COME VOYAGING WITH ME

Where are you now man of my love?
Listen to my song,
For I sing sad and low,
As the hours go,
Please come back to where you belong,
Husband, this is my song,
It's for you at home that I long.

Sail home soon, darling my love.
Ship no more on the sea,
For your wife does sigh,
Rant and cry.
Please come back, be more than a dream.
Husband I could scream,
It's for you at home that I dream.

Man, of mine, any woman in love,
Knows life and passion are now.
For us youth doesn't wait,
It's already late.
Please come back to hold me, then stay.
Husband I'm in such a way,
Oh, why do you leave anyway?

Of tomorrow's stuff, who cares my love.
Come home, how I hate you at sea.
For I'll kiss your lips,
I'll be your ships,
Please come home to a berth with me.
Husband I'll make it fun;
When you come voyaging---with me!!!!

Dreams

When a boy, awed by night's be-diamond sky,
He dreamed of life,
Of where and how he'd live.

In his youth, beneath pitch dark jungle canopy,
He dreamed of peace,
And where he'd go.

As a miner, laboring within a thousand feet of rock,
He dreamed of blue sky,
And how the sun would shine.

A lonely man, sitting in silent empty rooms,
He dreamed of a wife, of love,
Sharing and how they'd laugh.

The age-ed wreck, rocked upon a shady porch,
He dreamed, of God's paradise,
And how he'd earn his place.

Dust----below a life-less slab,
Not capable of dreams---of
And there is no longer the choice.
       One must act to make dreams come true.

FREE HAND

Was born a poor man, in a rich land.
Was a boat hand, was a ranch hand.
Was a rough neck, on a rig deck.
Wasn't one to suck up to the man.

I'm a lean man, not a mean man.
I'm a tough man, I'm a rough man.
Not a mad man, but I've got sand.
Ain't one to back down from the man.

For a man's life, it's a hard life.
For a man strife's, like a sharp knife.
It's the cutting what tests a blade.
Wasn't one to be made afraid.

On the short haul, on the long run.
On the hard days, get the work done.
I'm my own man, I'm a free hand.
Won't be one that's pushed by the man.
        Cause----Respect can't be held in the hand.

HER KISSES

In a depot, walking isles,
Searching countless shelves,
I must have seen a million things,
And still, what I remember now----
    Is that I saw her smile.

On a seaside, for a moon rise,
Walking down the dunes,
I must have seen a million stars,
And still, what I remember now----
    Is that I saw her eye's.

The congregation, did rejoice,
As they sang the holy psalm.
I could have heard a million notes,
And still, what I remember now----
    Is that I heard her voice.

Sitting, on the beach sand,
With her at my side,
I surely touched a million grains,
And still, what I remember now----
    Is that I touched her hand.

Life, its full of bliss's,
As we travel year on year.
I might have got a million gifts;
And still, what I remember now----
    Is that I got her----kisses

HOME

Upon a ribbon, concrete,
   multi jeweled asphalt, joining places, lands.
Upon this, crossing rivers,
   mountains, plains vast---I come.
Homeward upon bridge and causeway---
   pressing thru onrushing, pulsing glare.

You are before me---
   within the blurring flashes that assault my eyes.
You are before my mind,
   are my need, my goal awaiting.
Home to me, is where you are,
   it's your voice laughing, I hear.

Down the tunnel of night,
   drawn numb, behind luminous beams.
Down the familiar ways,
   encouraged, I struggle the last miles.
Now the dark house,
   climbing stiffly the steps, key turned, I enter.

Through the rooms,
   dim and silent, uncertain I move.
Through the hall,
   the door, softly speaking your name.
Up from slumber,
   your arms about me, murmurs of joy---

     Home I am, in these arms!
      Home is what you are for me!

          Home--

GOOD OLD DARRELL

Thinking of my buddy Darrell,
Side door Huey, combat apparel,
Saw the Nam along his M.G. barrel,
Sitting on his helmet to stay virile.

Joined up to get a medal for his girl,
A pretty thing, her name was Pearl.
Well what he got was an Army burial,
Joined up to get a medal for his girl,
A pretty thing, her name was Pearl.

Well, what he got was an Army burial,
And pretty Pearl----she married Earl.

I MUST DECLARE

You tell us lovely lady,
You have a troubling care,
That men should see you for yourself,
Instead they gawk and stare.

Well you could dress in baggy sweats,
Or chop and dye your hair,
Hide your face behind a mask,
But still you would be fair.

Now I am not the wisest man,
But truth I must declare.
Only God could love your mind...
And forget the rest is there..!

IDEA

The Muses tip toe through my brain,
Eye's roll back with airy strain.
The lights grow bright then wane.
My thought's I try to train.

I run for Pad an pen.
Jot down what's within.
Judge with frown or grin.
Genius---or---trash bin?

LOVE AND MARRIAGE

One evening at home and at leisure,
My daughter approached me.
Assuming me wise or at least knowledgeable,
She inquired concerning love, that most fickle
emotion.
She inquired concerning marriage, that most
ancient institution
She inquired of them wondering!

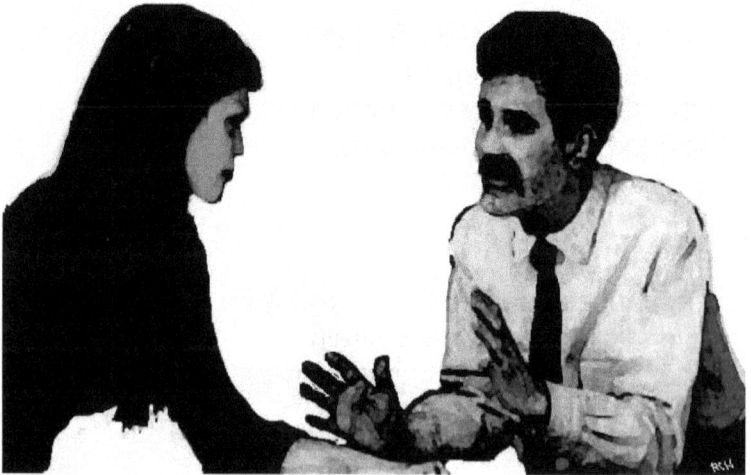

Wondering, what she might look for in it.
Wondering, what she might expect of it.
Wondering, about recognition of it.
Dealing with feelings of it,
Measurement, treatment, nurturing of it.
Wondering about marriage when she found it.
     All reasonable logical questions.
     Formed by an intelligent girl of sound mind.

But, how does one define love, when a thousand poets disagree?
How does one describe insanity?
How might she recognize it?
Lightning perhaps? Yes! Being struck by lightning. That might best describe love for you know it's around but won't see it coming.
Your knocked senseless, losing all control.
It hurts terribly and then you're numb.
After the shock it's pretty much up to chance whether you'll ever be normal again.

Love and lightning do strike more than once.
This is the serious romantic stuff were describing.
When it occurs, two persons should be involved,
with each other of course and at the same time.
Get the timing off and someone will be miserable.
And don't mistake lust or obsession for love.

Obsession is desire gone awry.

> A true love produces a mutual need to share.
> It's a shared comfort in each other's company.
> It's a shared pleasure in mutual endeavor.
> It's a shared misery caused by separation
> And a selfless concern for the others welfare.

The circumstances of love between a single and married pair differ vastly, for love and marriage is not the same thing at all.
Love is a strong but less than stable emotion.
Marriage is a formal commitment to obligation, an obligation understood between a man and woman, a pair, who have judged themselves and each other, as fit partners.

You may love a person, choosing to overlook flaws.
You may love a person for what they are.
You may accept any behavior they exhibit.
You may choose a non-judgmental form of love.
But if you choose to ignore serious flaws,
If you marry without using sound judgment,
You will consign yourself to painful failure.
Sharing your life with an irresponsible or faithless
partner for the sake of love, would be like a blind man
knowingly placing his trust----in a guide dog------
that has a penchant for chasing cars.

Love may be strong, but injury will emanate.

You see, love is a rush.
It's like a passion for a new car.
It's the style, color, comfort, the touch and smell.
You see yourself in it, changed, transported.

Marriage on the other hand is like buying the car,
And you'd best concern yourself with utility, durability
and price, because if what your buying into is not
dependable, you'll be left stranded in a marriage, a
marriage with an emotional cost that is too high to
maintain.

Lovers you see may be committed to each
other; spouses must be committed to the marriage.

Passion's cool, tastes change.
A love without formal obligation is in flux.

Marriage is an equal exchange, entered with a true
desire, the deep desire of warmly sharing one's self
with another.
It is recognition of commitment and promise of
loyalty; the presence of unquestioned trust,
between two equal, and loving friends.

Love and marriage when blended successfully,
love and marriage when maintained carefully,
creates the finest of human conditions.
It's well worth the work and compromise.

So, to her, to anyone, remember---love is a fine
madness but a good marriage---

It's a fine accomplishment.

OBEDIENCE

Each child has need to please parent.
Each child attempts to earn merit.
Most can't and become slowly errant.
Some can but the waste is apparent.
Could that be why..........?
Adam did,
Though God said, "dare 'ant"!!!!

LOVE IS AN OPEN HAND

He admired a glorious bird,
For her joyous song, he heard.
She soared free upon the air.
Knew no bounds at all,
Till, she perched upon his wall.

Because it pleased his mood,
He persuaded her with food,
Seduced her onto an open hand,
And that hand became a fist.
The bird was clutched, softly kissed.

He placed her in a cage quite fine,
A thing of craft his own design,
Placed a lock with his own hand.
He swore for the bird to care,
Brought her fruits, nuts and other fare.

The man gazed on this lovely bird,
Spoke his love with softened word,
Stroked her with gentle hand,
Loved how she would sing,
Loved the color of her wing.

From her cage, the man heard no song,
Had no sense of what was wrong.
He caressed her with his hand,
But could never understand,
When she never sang again----for---

    Joy springs from an open hand.

MARRIAGE IS

A marriage is not by vows of love,
By documents made.
What has it to do with a place, home,
Or things owned?
Old it is, old as the rhyme of life,
Old as creations mold.
For each compliments,
Each provides to the others need.
Each it serves, for it is in itself,
The serving of each other.
And other paramount to self,
Selfless thus satisfying.
Glad each in answering, out of self,
Thus, is hunger banished.
Each to each, the gift of self,
Union in blend of will.
By the joy of giving of one's self---
                    Is a marriage made---

MARRIED LIVING

Ah, young love, it's grand.
Oh; silly girl, foolish man.
Learn about it, firsthand.
What's married living?

Some good days, wild nights.
Some short cash, big fights.
Manpower, women's rights.
It's married living.

It's your dog, her cat.
It's ugly dress, stupid hat,
Old flames, nasty spats.
That's married living.

When laundry room, knee deep.
When kids sick, no sleep.
Light bills don't keep.
It's married living.

The tax refund, it's great.
The vacation trip can't wait.
In-laws arrive, just fate.
It's married living.

Her traffic fine, bum wrap.
His football bet, dumb sap.
Tough day, warm lap.
That's married living.

With loyal man, loving wife.
Faith and trust---doing right.
Hard work, good life----------JUST MARRIED LIVING.

53

MARS

I am the destroyer,
And to those who fail to flee me,
I am death.
I lick like flames.
Taste of me,.....

I am Hunger.

I am Fear,
And peace is no power to me.
I dine on hate,
Drink of injustice.
Taste of me,.....

I am Anger.

I am grief,
And the flesh of millions rot
To serve my cause.
Ashes are my bounty.
Taste of me,.....

I am Bitterness.

I am wrath,
And travel onward timeless,
Hammer cites into dust,
Trample joy and reason.
Taste of me with terror,.....

I am **War.**

MY PORCH

The house itself becomes much too dark.
Sometimes there's too much blare.
Other times its quite still, stark,
And so, my dear husband built my porch.

Sitting on it does not require coffee,
Or tea, not that I don't care,
For holding the hot cup of tea or coffee.
Waifing the aroma does please me, on my porch.

Coffee's aroma is of course not all I waif,
For I've hung flowers and ferns there,
From the rails and beams beside the door,
Where they look and smell good on my porch.

Wrapped in whatever, cup in hand I start the days',
Hidden among fragrant plants where,
Feet up on the rail I watch suns rays,
Creep under and over trees, onto my porch.

My daughter's cat, I think felt the same.
He lay peering out, four feet in the air,
Until one day, two stupid dogs came.
They burst up the steps, invading my porch.

Sylvester, "the cat was named that",
Recognized a bad situation there,
And ran for it but he was too fat.
He lost his ninth life fleeing my porch.

My son took him to the vet on a tray,
And we had hope, his condition being fair,
But it just didn't work out his way,
And now I miss him lounging on my porch.

Still rain or shine, day or night,
I feel peace and calm, when I rest and stare,
And it's nice alone, when avoiding fights,
Or even better getting over one, on my porch.

People walk by, or sometimes they stop.
We'll chat through ferns, out of glare,
Or I can speak over the rail top,
Smiling between my feet, on my porch.

My husband shares it, his chair by mine.
We have our best talks, lay things bare.
He travels and though I'm not one to whine,
I miss him, gone, when I'm on my porch.

Time passes, just like folks on foot-----slow.
He's due home soon from somewhere,
So, I sit cup in hand, watch flowers grow,
And when he arrives,
                    I'll greet him on my porch.

SLAVING

I'm slaving by the clock.
  I should have taken stock,
    Before I put myself in hock.

      I'm slaving by the clock.
        It's like a keyless lock,
          Shackled to a heavy rock.

        I'm slaving by the clock.
          Possessions, what a crock.
          This mess I'd like to chock.

          I'm slaving by the clock.
            The sound, it seems to mock.
            I work, tic, tock, tic, tock.

              I'm slaving by the clock.

MY RIGHT MAN

Just shopping around, it's already late,
With me at the height of my bloom.
Well now's the time at any rate,
To explain what I want in a groom.

When you reach this point of decision,
And of course, the fields so wide,
Every girl should have her own vision,
To help her to sort and decide.

My eyes would pick one that's handsome,
And to reach things, it helps if their tall.
Strength in a man, I can use some.
Yes! these traits, I insist on them all.

Oh! and then there's nobility, wisdom.
Yes! a serious thoughtful man,
But he has to be funny and joke some,
For a stick in the mud, I can't stand.

Sure, I want him playful and happy,
A big man, who's like a small boy,
But he should be sharp, snappy,
Someone you don't want to annoy.

He'll have to take charge, and guide me,
But will always do what I say,
And when I make him hate me,
He'll always love me anyway.

All of us women love shopping,
But I don't have to live at the mall.
He won't resent a little spending,
For he'll know I want him most of all.

Then to, I insist on an exclusive,
Loyalty being an absolute draw.
Another, I think is conclusive,
That fibbing is one major flaw.

On the matter of personal finance,
It helps if they come with some wealth,
But what counts is the level of romance,
Can he please and hold on to his health.

And I'm not adverse to a backrub,
But a full body massage is the way,
And I'd love to be sponged in a hot tub,
Any man who'd agree is okay.

When angry, cause I drive him crazy,
He'll make up before were to bed.
Then the subject will get really hazy,
And he'll please me crazy instead.

Oh yes, that's the guy I'll be wedding.
Alternates are not part of the plan,
And you'll all see the end of my pouting,
For the most pleasing life's the right man! ! ! !

OLD COURAGE

Aging, worn, short of possibilities, of self-respect,
　　I am adrift between interviews,
　　　　I hunt some illusive address.
　　　　　　The square found me,
　　　　　　　　Drew me to its cool center, it's fountain.

　　　　　　　I am moved.

He stands upon a masterful pile,
　　Of cut stone, cast bronze.
　　　　The slain, sprawl about him.
　　　　　Arms heavy, defiant,
　　　　　　　Even in torn, bloodied exhaustion,
　　　　　　The old warrior at bay.

Death crouches, foes closing, bent forward,
　　Relentless, restrained only by his fierce arrogance,
　　　Of eye, of stance; without doubt his time is near.
　　　　Death will prevail but by main force only.
　　　　　He will offer no compromise,
　　　　　　No heart half defense.

True to his life's course, you expect. . .
　　The very metal to rise straight,
　　　Struggle full force into them,
　　　　Cutting what path strength and courage allow.
　　　　He faces fate un-cowed.

Erect, determined----I pass on my way.

　　　　　He---with me.

Politics

Long winded speakers come out to us at night,
Say to us what's wrong---tell to us what's right.
George, Tom, Ulysses, a racists heritage, a blight.
Say the words you must, for you know were right?
Say, tear them down, hide the pieces out of sight

Say, burn down the nation, do it out of spite.
Say it you must, you know it's only right?
Superman's a fascists pig, Jesus, he's a honky.
Trust to us for all your needs,
Not to some Madonna on a donkey.

But when asked how---now we might eat,
They answer us with words so sweet.
Abide----someday you all will eat.
Yes, by and by,
In that glorious land above the sky.

But for now, just march and hey,
Riot for the things we say,
Vote for peace, we'll win the day,
Our government, for all will pay,
All for free; frees what we say.

Hear the news, they twist our way.
If needs to live hold you from the fray,
Listen now--- for we say,
You must live by eating hay.
You'll feast with us beyond election day.

And---you'll get your pie up in the sky,
But for that-----
You'll have to wait until you die.

RAIN SQUALL

Before a flickering bay of liquid silver moon, we are.
Above us the anvil of an evening squall.
Behind---a dark mass of trees,
Moss draped, shroud us.
Beside me, quiet save the brush of cloth.
You walk barefoot over cool sand.
The scent of you mingled with that of the shore,
It draws me.

As the moon clouds---deep shadow---alternates
With silent electric flash.
We together, turn toward our house,
Your hand you've placed in mine,
I, a guide as blind as you.
Still---on I lead, your body naked in my mind.
Our door is close as cool damp wind wraps us.
Trees bend---sound of thunders first crash.

From spattering rain, we scamper within,
Secure from the cool summer storm, you laugh low.
I pull the wet cloth of your blouse past your
shoulder,
Pressing my lips to your damp throat---embracing.
Rain drums urgently upon the roof.
Together, we sink to the floor,
Acknowledging the tumult, seeking each other.
Spent, calm, the storm, passes on its way.
                         Spent, ... we ...remain.

SAIGON SALLY

Saigon Sally, what a girl.
You're the countries second pearl.
When you took that cycle for a whirl,
All my buddy's hair would curl.

Oh Sally, what a treat,
As you raced up the street,
your machine guns flashing heat,
And the lead it sent to greet.

Hey Sally, you had style,
And I thought so all the while,
I dove behind that sandbag pile,
Being stung by shattered tile.

I remember being graced,
By the smile on your face,
As you sped past that place,
Tossing bombs with measured haste.

I can hear that cycle's roar,
As your satchel's blew the door,
And my buddies splattered gore,
Was spread across the hotel floor.

Though I think you really neat,
Too stave off such grim defeat,
I'll have to shoot you off your seat,
If again we chance to meet.

You know some thought you really vile,
And the troops, you sure did rile;
But myself-----speaking without guile,
Sally girl-----you sure had style. . .

THE SEA TUG

Out among the ocean storms,
Wind flays the mighty sea
Great foaming waves are marching,
Tops soaring off the lee.
The sea tug staggers onward,
Props churning doggedly.
Far aft on the hawser,
A tow drags heavily.

Too slow to run for harbor,
The tug holds on stubbornly.
She stays and takes her pounding,
As she battles fiercely.
Her bulwarks are far under,
Her deck scuppers never free.
A berth on an ocean tug,
Not an easy place to be.

The captain grips a sturdy rail,
As the decks slant drastically.
The helmsman staggers to his left,
The tug slew's off a lee.
Her bow goes plunging downward.
Winds mimic some banshee.
A comer lifts above the house.
It falls on them with glee.

The breaker slams the starboard.
Now a roll to port you'll see.
The crew they hold on tightly,
Midst the crash of crockery.
Suppers on the galley deck,
The good mate wears his tea.
A seaman tossed from off the head,
Is swearing angrily.

The engineers slip sliding,
Diesel soaked in misery,
Changing out fuel filters,
To prevent catastrophe.
For if his brutes should falter,
Needs no mystic to foresee,
The only one could save him,
Be the Lord of Galilee.

Like a shot, something parted.
Hear the captains stern decree.
It's the call, all hands-on deck,
And they don't go happily.
The nights all grey seas under.
Here they prove their pedigree.
A man might be swept away,
Or sliced in two or three. . .

The cold froth swirls about them,
And the works pure tyranny,
But soon the decks all ship shape.
In they stumble wearily.
High ships, or deep calm harbor,
To these comforts they would flee.
For the deck of a sea tugs,
Not an easy place to be.

Out among the blue grey storms

Where the wind rakes up the sea.

SHAPE SHIFTER

Jungle bases were not jungle,
Nearer Islands of desert,
Swallowed by endless oasis---olive drab.
Dust, dirt, sandbags, tents---olive drab
Ammo boxes, machines, weapons olive drab
The men were olive drab.
Some had stripes.
We imported everything but mud.
Mud--- it was domestic, as was our adversary,
He, being equally sucking, tenacious as the mud
We lived among them both.
Charlie, ever present, stuck to us, as did he did
VICTOR CHARLIE, using old machine guns.
Charlie, using bomb s made of our shell.
 Charlie fighting us above the camps,

Spying, killing, maiming -- same as us.
Victor Charlie -- like me -- a jungle beast.
For us both---this was country living in the
    sixties.
            It was not peaceful.

The farm, open, firm, cool snow, wheat.
The changeless seasons through,
Which like the golden corn I grew.
The Forty's, Fifty's, ever same un-dusted days
Of BB guns, pellet rifle's, the twenty-two.
Hunting, rats, rabbits, gofer, quiet I lay.
Patient hushed . . . site, breath squeeze.
A puff wait . . . site, and again I'd squeeze.
Few even knew, Bright eyed I watched.
I, the beaked, taloned bolt.
The Raptor that soared.
Few heard the fierce rush.
Few ever knew they'd died.
            Yet----It was peaceful.

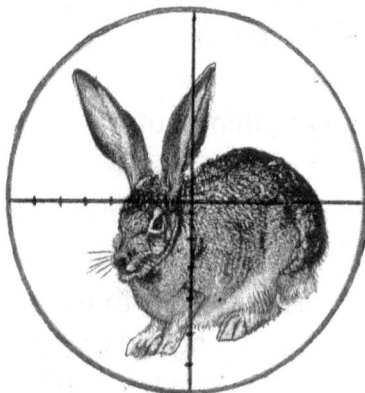

Skinned pelts sold.
The rabbits roasted, black from flames.
Spit over coals, crammed dripping, toasted,
Charred between my lips.
Within the child boasted.
Years grown, gone, civilized, marrying,
I'd become a horse, working, feeding,
In domestic boredom, sleeping, breeding.
The horse, how could it know, civil action---
Divorce---could transform it to a dog.
Loyal, obedient, fierce---
A focused fanged member of the pack,
Follower of a deep grooved track,
Follower of another's back.
I barked when appropriate.
                    It was not peaceful.

During this galvanic,
Machine like, marching, chanting,
We were given weapons---
For play slaying---
To aim at paper men.
Endless volleys were let off,
Resulting in slight casualties,
Suffered among the paper men,
Save my adversary's---with heart center holes.
Abruptly, a mark by my number---
My records on another stack.
Different beast, deadly value outside the pack.
They gave me another hat.
The dog became the cat.
Alone---waiting to choose---the sniper.
                    It was not peaceful.

I became a kind of Tiger.
I had a kind of stripes.
You can become a kind of anything . . ..
If you have the attitude.
I became a Tiger . . . developed the look.
People avoid you; you have the look.
A sight, a burning eye, you have power.
You have a jungle cunning.
You choose a place to wait.
You watch as they pass before you.
You can choose, do choose . . .
A tug at your shoulder, wait . . . wait . . ..
You can take your time, prowl, hide, wait.
You can choose again.
                    It was not peaceful.

They------provided the weapon, the sight,
They---the maps of distant mush,
Photos of politically favored prey,
They---sent me as a wandering demon,
Over hills of evening twilight------
Bearing death-----
As casually as the postman----
With--- a pouch of junk mail.
Through the rifle scope,
A thousand-yard smile is near-----
A grimace of fear, of anger, is near-----
So many faces, near, too near.
The face of the lovely young girl,
The old man, a boy, soldiers all----
I'd have much sooner killed rabbits.
Her face-----Her smile----are with me still.
　　　　She relaxed as she fell . . ..
　　　　　　　　It was not peaceful.

Demon,
        Tiger,
                Slayer,
                        Prowler of day and dark.
I . . .. with the cat stripes,
The cold fire, the attitude,
They spoke to me strangely, avoiding my eye.
Looking at them, I saw her face,
Her hair dangled over one eye.

They avoided my eyes.

The stripes were cracks,
Fissures in my attitude,
I looking, looking,
As he passes before me to be chosen.
His face, confident, strong----at me, peering,
From the near-----
              One----
                  thousand----
                      yards----
                          waiting----

      And-----she relaxed as she fell.

Four segments of his perspiring youthful face,
Are before my crystal eye.
Flesh that may still live.

      And-----she relaxed as she fell----

          I------fired high.
            The Tiger vanished.
                It-----was peaceful!

SHARE THE MOMENT

A winter night but soft . . .
Droplets of light fall through . . .
Great oaks crowding the shore.
Drips of Moon splash us,
We go as if swimming among living patterns,
In the deep pools of dark, clouds coming, going,
Even as we, before a bright Moon.

At my side, embracing my arm,
Your face presses my shoulder.
Reflection parades the bay as our feet.
A flickering shadow sky----
Lost beyond trees, children slumber,
They dream in the dim warmth of our home.
Here, upon water, grass, leaves,
Wind plays for us---trees sway in rhythm.
We, within the dancing beams of light,
Share hand in hand the moment.
        I kiss your glistening eyes.
            We cling beneath the stars.
                For---my unit leaves ... tomorrow.

SHE DANCED FOR HIM

In mighty Nineveh, long since become dust,
Maids fresh were beckoned, by Nash-de-ust,
Where before his throne and eyes of lust,
Performed in thinnest vials, their breast out thrust,
And sought with youthful grace his couch in trust.
        Oh, they danced for him, only him.

Deep jungle primal, clearing still unfound.
Child is made woman, see-- her hair is bound.
Men close the circle, sacred drums, they sound.
Her eye's wide searching seek him all around.
See how she walks, so proudly to his ground,
        Then she danced for him, only him.

Neath silken tent, on dust blown desert scape,
At feast her Lord drank deeply of the grape.
With clap of hand he bids her from back of drape,
Before their eyes, and blushing sheds her cape.
Obedient, she bows as his strangers' gape,
        Then she danced for him, only him.

Beside the wide plaza, on the end of day,
Rests proudly the young, Matador, El Rey.
He sips hot, dark wine, hears the music play,
Heart full with passion, she glides his way,
For she caught fire as he fought today,
    Now she danced for him, only him.

On their street, houses glow, light shifts the air.
Sports again tonight, she hates the blare.
Being lonely with him here, is it fair?
He's her man, she can have him, will she dare?
Cloths fall, he sees she's wearing only hair,
    Then she danced for him, only him . . .

RED WINE

Red wine, red wine,
Look misery.
Red wine I drink,
Then dwell on thee.

Useless it seems,
Wedded to thee,
Then oft away,
Oh lonely sea.

Wild were the nights,
Dear wife for me.
Sweet your delights,
Our wanton spree.

Sore is my heart.
Sour is the wine.
Why did I depart,
Young love of mine.

Done with the ship.
Done with the sea.
Done with red wine.
Soon I drink of thee.

SHE SINGS THE PUPPY-CAT

OH . . . .
I like who I am.
I'd like you to know.
I'll burst like a dam,
So away we go.

I like being good.
I like being sweet.
I like what I should,
But my rooms never neat.
I like my school.

I like my fun
   I like to be cool,
      When I play and run.

I like to listen.
   I like to read.
      I like fussing,
         And no work, I plead.

I like cooking.
    like my cake.
        I like messing.
            It's so fun to bake.

I like to be funny.
I like to be fair.
I like it sunny,
And I love a dare

I like warm puppies.
And I like fat cats.
I like being snoopy
And I love big hats

I like to giggle.
  I like to laugh.
    I like to wiggle,
        And play in the bath.

I like to tickle.
  I like squirm.
    I like to squiggle,
        Like a little worm.

I like to snuggle.
　I like to curl.
　　I like to cuddle.
　　　I'm a warm little girl.

　　　　I like family.
　　　　　I like my home.
　　　　　　I like to be happy,
　　　　　　　Just like this Poem.

WE CHANGED

Upon a glowing lavender blue night,
The white mane d waves rush to spend their might.
Above seabirds' circle, flash thru starry light.
As we watch from dunes, ships dance out of sight.

The ocean rolls its body on the strand.
Silver flecked, 'neath our feet, the velvet sand.
Entranced, two strangers, walking hand in hand,
Our tattered cautious hearts opened, filled and

Your misty moon lit face began to care,
Pale, framed in the golden halo of your hair.
You gazed up at me with a look so rare,
A look I'd hoped and dreamed but never dared.

Our tracks below us, frozen in the sand,
Hearts cast as one, in hallooed moon, we stand.
A trembling moment, in a timeless land,
Love took us, touched our lives, we changed!

SIDEWALK

We spent a lot of time on this sidewalk.
From its curb we had sat in the cool mornings,
Our eyes feeling the sunrise
Our expectations of another day
And there I was in its shady parts,
In the late afternoon, …. lonely,
Watching the people,
Go about their routines.
Then came the evening
As we all congregated …..
On our little strip of cement
With our music our drinks
The shadows growing with our drunk,
The chill of the evening would settle down
And I would feel the heat ….. still held within.

R.S Horton

SMITTEN

When first he saw her, she seemed sparkling
mystery.
A dream unmatched in recent history.
A visage lite by twilight's starry pyre.
Kindling clothed in dancing fairy fire,
To draw him----gladly mad by nameless grace,
To seek in her his dwelling place.

Forth, not boldly but as a pilgrim he,
Ventures on distracted odyssey.
Not normal man but fool, impaired of reason,
Ardently comes on, careless of the season.
Unarmed, thru forest tangled, wholly lost,
Pursues confused, at any cost.

And with stupid courage, with awkward charm
With her conversing, avoids alarm.
Thus, with words not sane but eloquent,
He swears she flesh but heaven sent.
Wrapped in raptures rage, he raves away!
She grins at him---------and lets him stay.

STATE OF MIND

Cool sunshine, striding by she goes.
Long legged, lithe, she almost flows.
Heads turn, caught by her subtle grace.
Quick toss swings glossy hair in place.
Memories are haunted by her face.
Who'd guess her hearts a rocky space.
And she won't let anyone see in.

Not in the state of mind she's in!

Gentile child, now this woman rare.
Don't know how she got from there to here.
Young thing was daddy's perfect girl.
Romance struck her with a dizzy whirl.
Now her hearts like a glassy pearl.
Pain sealed up in layered curl.
She can't tell what's locked within.

Not in the state of mind she's in.

Best wife, a marriage and a home.
Love match, until he choose to roam.
Good girl became the devil's bride.
Broke dream, he mocked you and he lied.
You gave him love with all your might,
But he made the good things seem not right.
She don't know how to fight and win,

Not in the state of mind she's in.

Shades pulled she dances through the night.
What the lady feels, she can't fight.
Cold flash of anger deep and bright,
Takes another drink to make it right.
Face holds a hint of something wild.
And wine won't heal the little child,
But she don't intend to hurt again.

Not in the state of mind she's in.

Just right job, busy, that's her style.
Loneliness last a little while.
Keeping to herself, so its denial.
It sure beats a man by a mile.
But then she trembles deep within.
Lady, life alone 's just a sin,
But she's not ready to give in.

    Not in the state of mind she's in.

Held fast girl, when you might have run.
Could this new man be the real one?
Show him your confidence and charm.
Rich laugh smile warmly on his arm.
Praying, you won't come to any harm.
Hidden is the little girls alarm,
For she's afraid she might lose again,

    Now in the state of mind she's in.

Shy heart, you've promised to belong.
This one, he's steady, this one's strong.
If you feel pleasure, what's so wrong?
You've heard love's song, so come along,
And woman trust, for trust can save.
Open up and give the love you gave.
And maybe now she'll be that brave again,

    Now, in the state of, the state of mind she's in.

STRIKE OUT FOR THE LIGHT

Swallowed by the sea,
Of voices drowning me,
By the world destroyed,
By dark and sucking void,
Deep by dragging weights,
Demands of loves and hates,
Clutched by clinging souls,
By those never whole,
Those who cannot swim,
Those who never sought,
Those begging to be taught,
Those crying to be brought.
I struggle up to breath,
Hear screams all very near,
Of which one voice is clear,
It is my own I fear.
I listen to its call,
There is no choice at all.
I strike out for the light,
To save the only life I might.

SURE

Are the things you know suspicions?
Perhaps you merely guessed'
Shouldn't you make sure,
Before choosing to detest.

SUCCESSIONS

Generations, patterns, swells upon the shore,
The timeless march, waves of life, of more,
Spaced, the one behind, the one before.
Generations same. . . . might have we been more,
Than those ahead we saw. . . . . .
When they rose, to fall upon the shore?

Before me, glimpses, sightings, just a few.
Old ones who went before us through,
Spaced just ahead, even some we knew,
Sought the false, while others held the true.
What will we hold, you and I . . . .
When we rise to fall upon the shore?

Father before me, the one I walk behind,
His examples were my first design's.
Spaced near I saw the course, the fine,
Who he was, which traits I'd choose as mine,
The parts of him that will be me . . . .
When I rise to fall upon the shore?

Before my sons, I rise upon the shore,
Exposed, the good, the bad, the sore.
Spaced behind do they deplore,
Any bad, while all my good they store,
To be better men than I . . . . my sons,

When they rise to fall upon the shore?

THE LEARNING BOAT

Wood hulled, island built, her sail a droop,
Just bought, clumsy, an old sloop,
Ghosts Nor-thard on the streams warm back,
Low ahead, dark clouds begin to stack.
The Man, weathered, burned of tropic suns,
His feature's lined by years of ocean runs,
Choose the boat to teach, not to hamper,
A disappointed son in sullen temper.
Difficult a craft as could be had,
Not the type of boat to please the lad.

A glassy Western Sun wanes forth.
While bar clouds climb dark to the North.
No air moves to make the rigging sing.
No ripple save the gulls dipped wing.
Smooth swells roll, softly heave.
Unsure zephyrs gush, gasp to breath.
Mirthful malice in the sea resides,
Ever changing, patient, it abides.
Airs shift, rounding, Nor-ward veer,
Knowing no haven port lies near.

Dolphins breach, then blowing, glide nearby,
While seeming to inquire why.
Perhaps statements of wise learning's,
Comments on prudence and observings.
Watched by the boy, dolphin seem to play,
Un-spoke the Man hears what they say.
Those on the current of the stream,
Wind to the North, no happy dream.
Gaze beyond the heads'ls, well he knows,
Waits slouched, for now soon it blows.

Wet air shakes the sail, fitful slaps.
Cat's paw's claw up the first white caps.
Sloop cants, heels, her rudder churns;
Sargasso parts to swirl astern.
Of ominous change, the boys aware,
But assured of the Man's calming stare;
Watches dolphin darting to and fro,
Until they fade and vanish deep below.
A weakened Sun, to the west, sinks down;
The black seas steepen all around.

Scent of rain upon the wind is high,
First spray wets what once was dry.
The boy obeys, quick drop the jib!
It drapes the prow like a baby's bib.
He drags it in to make secure,
Hears, take the time son, make it sure,
Then close up, seal tight the hatch,
Free the pump and tie the latch.
The shrouds are taut, they start to hum.
Winds veer a point and harder come.

The sloop rail under, plows ahead,
Nor-wind howls at canvass hard.
Then plunging dips it's bows instead.
Nor by East reads the compass card.
They together fight and reef the main,
Eye's stung by the driving rain.
Far oft the bow, from out of gloom,
Faintly glows the beacon's pale loom.
Piercing comes the light's first flash,
Blotted by a breaker's sodden crash.

Reaching, the sloop goes beam to every wave,
Goes madly whipped, as driven slave,
Staggering under thoughtless blows,
Specked foam and sea across her flows.
Beneath his hand, by his will she lives.
All the hard-taught lore he has, he gives.
Comer abreast, pinch up to the gusts,
Heeled sharp, he hopes the mast don't bust.
The boy cast on a sea that he knows not,
Clings to the coaming, pumping till he's hot.

Bearing down, the wave upon them raced,
Boards and swamps them to the waist.
The sloop swept sideward far to lee,
Shakes the froth and struggles free.
Braced at the helm, straight as a staff,
The man roars out a hearty laugh,
Tucks the tiller tight, up to his chest,
And surfs before a tumbling crest.
The boy sees him as a different man,
As he fights the sea to gain the land.

Dark shadowed earth beyond the spray,
Above sweeps the light to guide the way,
Reflects wet skin, his father's teeth an eye,
As through the jetty's fangs they fly.
Rain and scud, each the other crowds,
Electric columns lift the clouds,
As flung spume, as seabird swooping,
They pass 'neath light's beam looping.
In quiet water, sails rifle crack . . .
As they jib around for one last tack.

Sheets cast off writher, thrash like snakes.
Halyards loosed, her last sail she slakes,
And slides to bump the wharf's high lee,
Come snug to rest upon the pier head tee.
Silent the boy, then reverent, low----
She's seaworthy dad----I didn't know.
Salt stiff, his father's face, it smiles.
The lines of his eyes could measure miles.
He looked upon the frail sloop; he stood----
You'll soon learn son, and well you should,

Skills in the man----

Not the wood.

THE NIGHT

Quiet. . .. the enveloping night---save. . .
  the whisper of breath, somnolent beside.
    Humid the evening had been.
Shed linen reveals his long bare form.
  Last glimmers of dampness dry,
    As her smile wanders familiar contours.
      He is hers

Restless----she rises, drifting. . . .
  with fluid grace through dim purple rooms,
    only to return----restless still, to his bed.
On her side, reclining,
  long hair spilled across his abdomen,
    cheek upon it, calm, content.

Rhythmic the surge of breath. . . .
  reminiscent of ocean swell, lulls her.
    Absently a finger traces.
Tender patterns, faintly brushing,
  twirling the dark hair of pubis, thigh.
    Random, as a child might etch in sand.
      He is hers.

Subtle the change----minute,
   a pulse beneath ear, temple.
     In intimate, mirthful awe she watches.
Passion's Phoenix rises.
   Fingers to her lips, press back the smallest laugh.
     Hesitantly reaching, she touches, caresses.
       He is Hers.

Air faint with the scent of hyacinth cools.
   Curtains lift----fall.
     Her face tilts, nuzzles her warm pillow.
Emboldened---her tongue tickles his stomach.
   Hard muscle contracts, spasms,
     roused, yet he sleeps.
       He is hers.

Slumbering carnal power channels
   vision, flesh, blood meld to a focus,
     a vortex. . . .at her very center.
Clenching amidst waves of fever chill,
   knees press inward.
     Trembling, she twists, knees, hesitant,
obsessed.

Memory's flash, she a girl, meadow, wind.
   Mounted upon the shivering energy of a Hunter.
     Images flood consciousness.
Reality mingling within the imaginary.
   Rush of dark blurred landscape. . . .
     her borne on rippling strength.
       He is hers.

Curtains billow out, dance above the bed.
  Desire burns, draws.
    Compulsion overcomes restraint.
Fearful----expectant----
  she swings astride him gently . . . .
    arched, chin high, in a single gasping slide.
      He is hers.

He moves ... below, within, yet he sleeps.
  Tender she bends to kiss, breasts brush his chest.
  Knees press, gripping, she moves.
Slow as a rider posting, gathering,
  quickened as the timeless rhythm takes her.
    High, free, she raced the moon.

Stars stream past to burst,
    explode behind her eyes.
      Blind---rhythm lost midst sudden upheaval.
Thrown tumbling, crushed beneath, held helpless.
  For breath, struggling in panting liquid passion,
    pacing, falters. . . .
Possessed, trembling, spent, she succumbs.
  Limp, languid, sated, curls child-like,
    with half murmurs, curls, within, without,
      In warm slumber----She is his..

Quiet----the enveloping night. . . .
  save her soft breath.
    He propped, resting on elbow, studies her hair,
Pleasantly bewildered, a short laugh springs out.
  He lies back---now sleepless---he gazes upon her.
    Woman---Wife---Mystery,
        She is his

The Wind

Cobalt blue sky, white cloud wisp---
    above the wind---wind---the wind---
Blue black sea' white foam from turquoise bursts---
    below the wind--- wild---wind----.
Tan specked sand, un-warmed of autumn sun'
    drifts-- before the wind--- wind--- the wind---
We snug, entwined, our sleeping bag ripples'
    in the wind--- cold--- wind---

We watch waves dash, crash upon the shore,
    waves driven by the wind--- wind---the wind---
Lather froths, pressed to the sand,
    trembles, in the wind----
Gulls screaming, soar
    on the wind--- wild---wind.

Sea oats whipping, lash the dunes,
    as we lay whispering of the wind--- wind---wind--
-
 Kiss, sighing murmurs of love,
   While wrapped in the wind--- jealous wind---

Sun yellow, sun orange, burgundy, gone.
    All dark, beneath the wind--- cold--- wind---
Lights beckon cross grey purple sand,
    Running we, amidst the wind--- cruel--- wind---

Laughing doors receive us,
   slam against the wind----.
Without howls the wind---,
    Moans the cold, lonely wind---,
       the wind----wind----wind----wind----wind----wind.

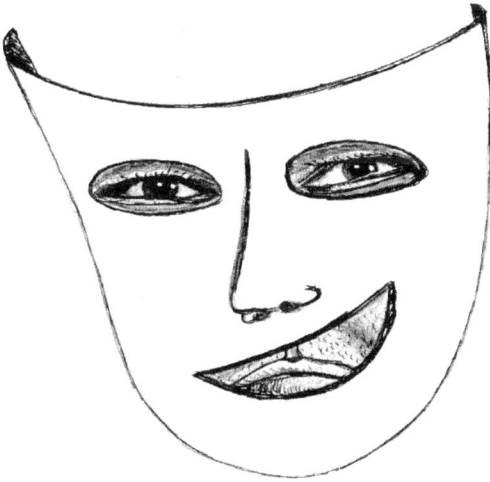

They

Oh, we all know of hate,
But it's menace is concealed.
Some of us must dominate,
But they won't be revealed.

Oh, we all know they're here,
But their skill is masquerading.
When the danger grabs us,
It's too late to be afraid.

Some need a world of strife,
With deceit and hate they rise.
Others bind a single wife,
To beat and terrorize.

Oh, we all know they're here,
But we only know the actors.
The face they are projecting is,
For them the major factor.

They cloak themselves with charm,
Convince us there's no danger,
But if you touch the mask,
You'll meet the vicious stranger.

Oh, we all know they're here,
And we look at one another.
We see Hitler's and Stalin's but
More often husbands, fathers.

And they all must have slaves,
They must grind them in the mire.
And if you are in bondage,
You learn what they require.

Oh, we all know they're here.
They deceive and they devour.
They are the puppet masters.
And yet within they cower.

They learned that love meant hurt,
And pity meant reviling.
They were the tortured children,
Now they do the torturing.

Oh, we all know they're here,
And their fear is the destroyer.
They abuse without remorse.
They spend to be your buyer.

For they're always right,
And if they're wrong there's a reason,
For insides a hunted child,
Who avenges every season.

Oh, we all know they're here.
We can fight or serve their demon,
But we can never change them,
It's suffer, fight, or run.

For their life is a stage.
We don't see behind the curtain,
We don't always see the monster,
But we see his victims bleed.

Oh, we all know they're here,
But with them, there's no relating.
They just make us feel guilty,
They can't help manipulating.

And we can't ever trust,
For their words they don't honor.
We can't help or compromise,
It's only suffer, fight, or run.

SHUT THE WINDOW

The still black night echoes …
The hopeless sobs of a woman.
Frantic cries…..anguished,
So helpless, so wrenching ….
A man beating a woman.

Deep drunken anger….. muffles ….
The shrieks of a woman.
Soft, fearful whimpers,
Of small children watching ….
A father beating a mother.

Slam of a window……….. dulls…
The muffled screams of a woman.
Gasping sobs, bewildered,
Sweaty fists thudding….
He's only beating his woman.

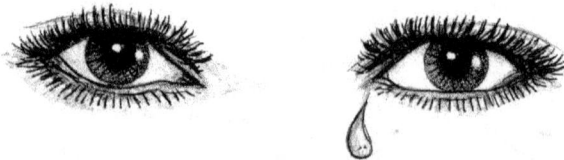

TREASURE

There upon the low Guiana coast,
Where the Demerara River dies,
Lie the swarming delta swamps,
Great clouds of birds, of butterflies.

In the squalled slums of Georgetown,
How the muddy river stank,
I built the boats of rough-cut wood,
Went upstream close to it's bank.

Laconic, black eyed Indios,
Muscles flexed as south we bore,
Beneath a wild jungle's canopy,
Where bright winged rainbows soar.

Diamonds lay above the falls,
Six hundred winding miles and more,
There below a gorge's rocky walls,
Within the old volcano's core.

We hacked and sweat up current,
To that place I'd come to dive,
Neath the black and muddy waters,
Where starved Piranha thrive.

Each day I sought a fortune,
Kept the terror tightly checked,
With courage, I dove dawn to noon,
Each plunge riches I'd expect.

I clawed the pebbled bottom,
As the river current swirled.
Ah, those uncut rocks, I found them,
Hauled them up into the world.

When the time of rains was finished,
River waters fell away.
The Indians simply vanished,
Choosing from the stores their pay.

Alone I packed my gear up,
Packed my bag of shinny stones,
Climbed West into the mountains,
Misty green volcanic cones.

I walked deep jungle valleys,
Marched the cloudy, high plateaus,
Saw the lost and hidden places,
Man don't see and never knows.

I was frozen, then I sweltered,
The machete grew to my hand.
I cut my way across the sky,
Back to where structures shape the land.

There, amidst a market's noisy push,
I sold my glossy stones,
Bought a ride on medal wings,
To a world of factories and phones.

These years I've toiled within walls,
Worked my sets of hours, of days,
Breathed air foul with soot that falls,
In veils of sickly grays.

At night as urban streets begin to crawl,
The frantic cities writhes and wails.
I sigh---for I'd once known such wealth.
Secret---My misty jungle streams,
        I still see them---In my dreams.

WALLS

There was once an open door;
What was hers was mine and more.
There was no doubt before;
Being one, in love, amour.

One day I sensed a key,
For a door that once swung free;
Nothing I could see.
She was confusing me.

Of walls that now reside.
When did her mood grow cool?
An inflection of some rule.
Was she meaning to be cruel?

Uncertain, I felt a fool.
All night, here by her side,
The pull of passions tide;
Held back by fear inside,

STRANGE

One day she seemed to change,
As if I'd got the mange.
Everything became so strange.
Could I be deranged
One day she simply changed.

SUN

Sun, flaming engine,
God of Pagan man.
Draws moisture of the sea upon the land.
It lights, it warms with gold array,
And conjuring up the winds,
Sends them reeling off away

SEA

Ageless, trackless mother to us all,
Tempts her lover's to her,
Woos them with a siren's call.
Fortunes, far horizons,
Life to make the spirit soar,
But show a single weakness . . . .
She'll drink you with a roar.

WHAT AM I?

A shadow with no casting
I look at myself and see others
What do I expect?
To look in their eyes, into their souls
And draw out some truth,
Truth I cannot find on my own.
All I find is ......others
They......
As lost in these empty questioned as I
But I know as many times
As I am disappointed
I will continue to repeat,
Like someone looking for a misplaced possession
Keeps searching the same doors,
Again, and again ... hoping ...maybe

They just glanced over it.

R. S. Horton

What ?????????????

What do we know,
Or, have we only guessed ?
What if with the facts,
Were not really blessed ?
What do we learn,
And is it for the best ?
What we believe is true,
How was it impressed ?
What are we teaching,
What is it we stress ?
What I do not know,
This I can confess !
What is doubt for?
A question to address ?
What is truth to you,
Is my truth the less ?
What could end the muddle,
Facts bluntly wrest ?
What can clear the mist,
Clean up all the mess ?
What you think is true!
Can you answer yes ?
What the secrets are,
It's creations jest !
What if we climb high,
Stand upon the crest ?
What do we seek?
Face we East or West ?
What is your truth and,
Should we burn the rest ?
What is each man's truth?
Will it pass the test ?

WHISKEY JOE

What became of Whiskey Joe?

Of him, who but me remembers,
Joe out on mangrove point,
Among the rotting timbers,
His fleet of salvaged treasure.

Am I the last who remembers,
That not much of Joe was pure?
He drank and seldom bathed,
Was unshaved and stank for sure.

I guess only I remember,
Joe's dream of a sailing tour.
The county Sheriff burned him out,
More loss than he could endure.

And yet, who but me remembers,

He was more than some old cur.
Joe once had a family, had a life,
Had a mother, and a wife.
I once swapped his son a knife.

Joe---what ever happened to your life?

MEMORY'S

During a holiday evening,
Among friends and family,
I overheard her, telling, relating,
To her sister, of some past event,
Of a time, place and happening,
We had shared as man and wife, together.
How differently I had looked
Upon my memory of it.
She and I had known and lived
Those moments side by side,
Yet our understanding of them
Seemed so very separate.
Imperfect overlays of the pattern
Of our personal history.
Similar, yet differing as one's
Adventure seems the other's trial.
One's reflection of triumph or humor,
The other views as failure, humiliation.
How strange that it had never occurred to me,
This concept of perception.
Reality and fact, bent to multiple
Versions that are equally true.
In retrospect I must suppose

All life and history are so.
What takes place midst the group,
Is the same but not perceived so.
All share in the moment,
But each is shaped differently by it.
Each samples with a unique pallet,
Of his or her own, the fare.
Each views out of strength or fear,
Not apparent to others.
Separately each of us is affected
According to our place in things.
One may cause anger,
Another is consumed with that anger
My daughter suffering a hurt,
Recalls not what my wife, who soothes her.
My arrant son, whom I punish,
Has recollections quite different from me.
Neither experiences the mixed loyalties,
That beset the wife and mother.
All the tales, stories, remembrances
Of our collective lives are truth.
Our emotions, images, our words are truth,
But distinguishable separate truth.
We share so much,
Share all that is possible to share.
Husbands, wives, families, associates,
All the world forms circles.
The events of our lives
Take shape within these circles,
And each records truth at center ring,
From a place-----
        Where only one----**can see.**

Dedicated to my father, *E. E. Horton*

Stop and smell the roses.
My father's advise

www.ingramcontent.com/pod-product-compliance
Lightning Source LLC
Chambersburg PA
CBHW061743020426
42331CB00006B/1340